ART MAKES PEOPLE. POWERFUL.

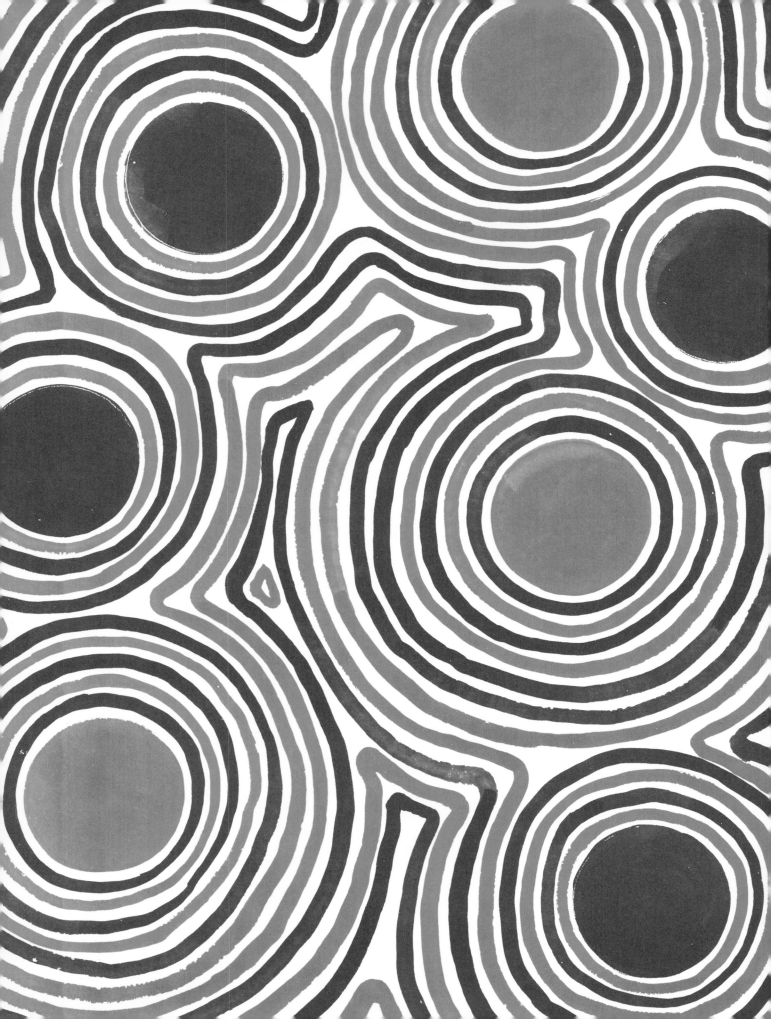

ART MAKES PEOPLE POWERFUL

Bob and Roberta Smith

WIDE EYED EDITIONS

HELLO!

I am Bob and Roberta Smith

Nice to meet you!

I AM AN ARTIST. AND SO ARE YOU!
I know that we can all make art, and when we
do it is very powerful!

I like making art because it can do so many
things. It can help you show things
you don't know how to say.
It can make you laugh!
It can help you imagine a different world
and it can remind you how beautiful
the world already is. It can help you
make new discoveries.

ART IS VERY POWERFUL
AND SO ARE YOU.
NOW LET'S MAKE SOME
POWERFUL ART TOGETHER.

WELCOME TO MY BOOK

Here are the things we'll discover and explore inside it:

1. IDEAS ARE POWERFUL

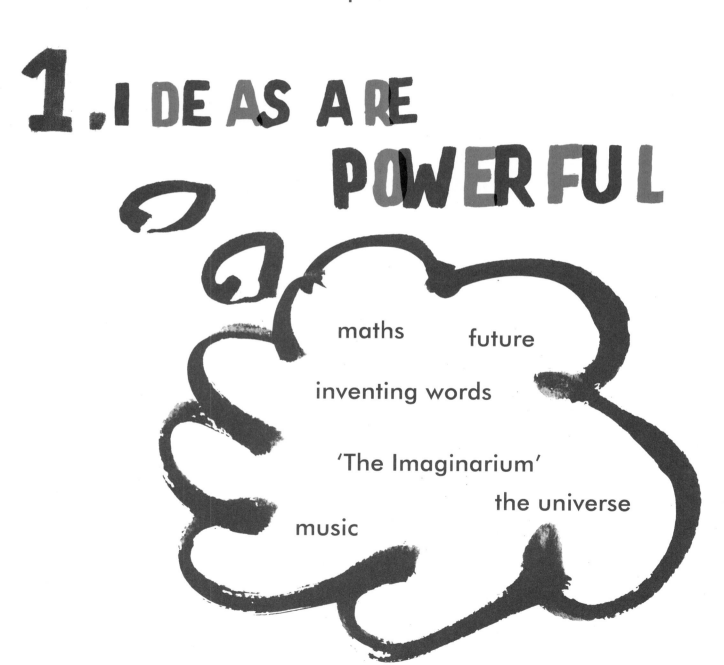

maths

future

inventing words

'The Imaginarium'

the universe

music

2. PLAY IS POWERFUL

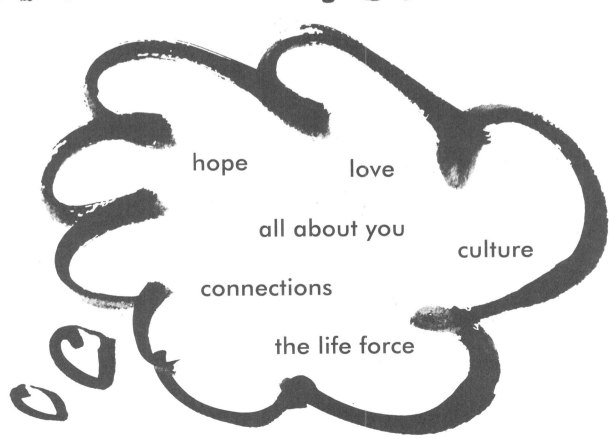

topsy-turvy

making marks

shapes

colour

fonts

patterns

3. PEOPLE ARE POWERFUL

hope

love

all about you

culture

connections

the life force

a book by

BOB AND ROBERTA SMITH AND YOU!

How does art make you **powerful**?
We'll start at the beginning by painting the
big bang and thinking about the imagination.

Then we explore the secret to a good life…
(which is having the right **pencil)**. We'll explore all the
wonderful things this that magic tool can do.

Then we'll **paint ourselves**, what we look like
but also what we like to do.

After that we'll take a trip to the **shape invention
centre** to make some new things and then finally we
return to '**The Imaginarium**' to dream up the future.

Bob and Roberta Smith has devised this book
for children, but in reality it is an activity
book for **everyone**.

YOU CAN PAINT AND DRAW IN THIS BOOK

START RIGHT THERE

Don't be shy – draw all over this
page to warm up your pencils and paints.

NICE!

CHAPTER 1.

IDEAS ARE POWERFUL

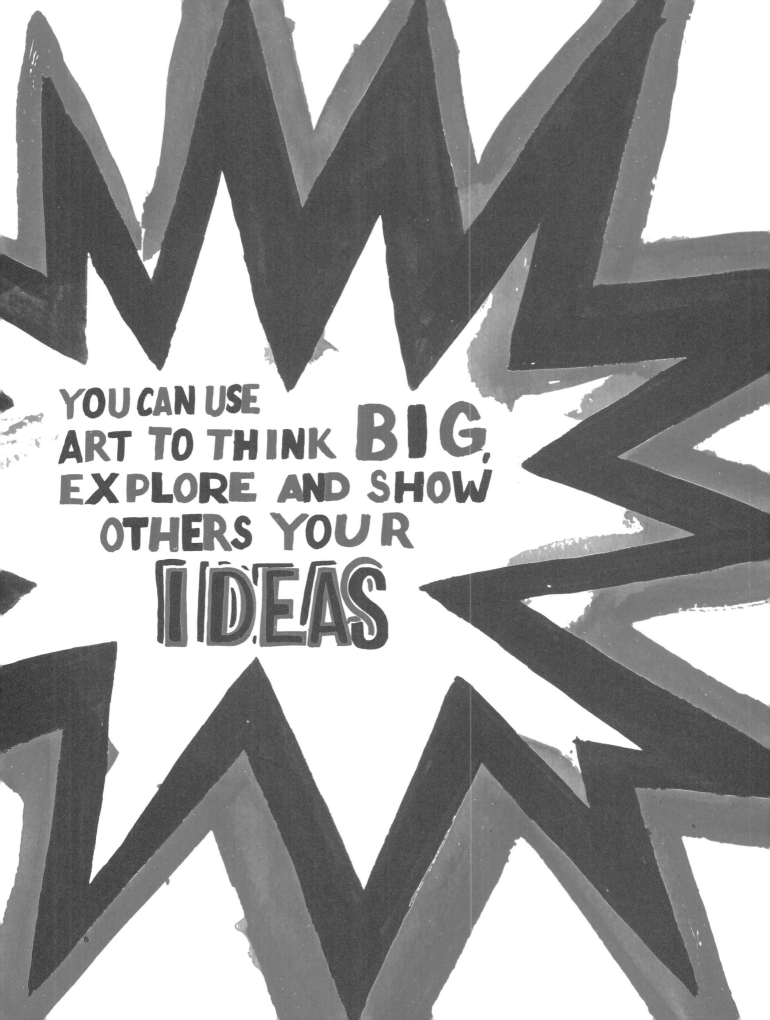

LET'S START AT THE BEGINNING

WHAT DOES A BEGINNING LOOK LIKE?

The universe started as a giant ball of matter –
draw a giant blob on this page.

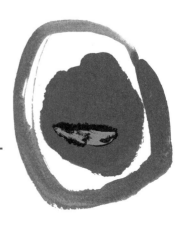

PAINT THE
BIG BANG

THAT BEGAN THE UNIVERSE

What does your blob look like as it explodes?

LET'S PAINT THE UNIVERSE

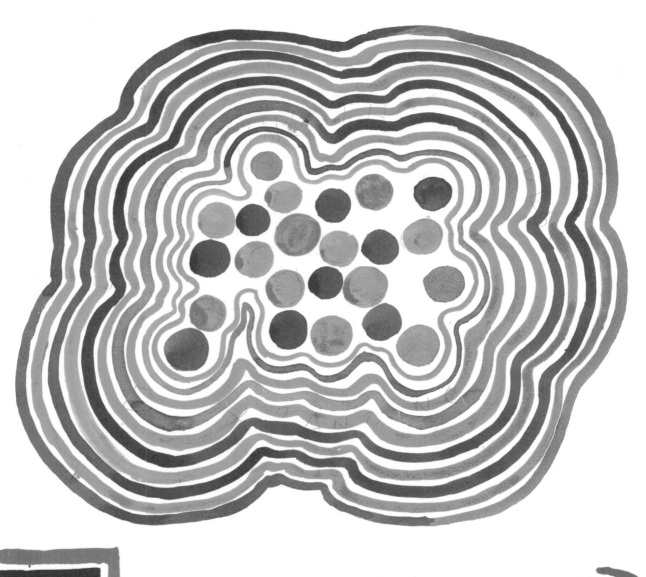

EXPANDING

Continue painting the great expansion...

WHAT DOES LIFE LOOK LIKE ON OTHER PLANETS?

THAT LOOKS
AMAZING!

SEE IF YOU CAN FIT THE WHOLE UNIVERSE ON HERE

WHAT GOES ON BEYOND THE UNIVERSE IS WITHIN YOU. IT'S CALLED THE

IMAGINATION

THE IMAGINATION IS IN HERE

BETWEEN THE EARS

Draw what's between your ears.

USE IMAGINATION TO THINK
DEEPER

MONDAY

TUESDAY

WEDNESDAY

THURSDAY

FRIDAY

SATURDAY

SUNDAY

NEXT WEEK'S BLOBS →

THIS IS HOW MY WEEK LOOKS IN BLOBS

HOW DO YOU PICTURE TIME?

Paint a blob for each day of the week, or paint time your way.

USE PAINT TO GET IDEAS OUT THERE

Use these placards to paint
messages you want to tell
the world.

THE SECRET TO A GOOD LIFE IS TO GET A GOOD PENCIL. A 2B OR A 3B (NOT AN HB, THOSE ARE FOR ARCHITECTS)

THE WORLD

Experiment using different pencils on the page.

IMAGINE YOURSELF IN THE FUTURE

This is me. I think I'm always destined to wear a hat.

Draw what you might look like in the future here.

OR REMEMBER YOURSELF IN THE PAST

WHAT WILL THE

Art helps us design the future, what will the place you live in look like?

FUTURE LOOK LIKE?

MAKE THINGS UP

Your imagination doesn't have to obey the universe's rules. It's that powerful.

Draw something impossible.

I LIKE YOUR THINKING

INVENT NEW COLOURS

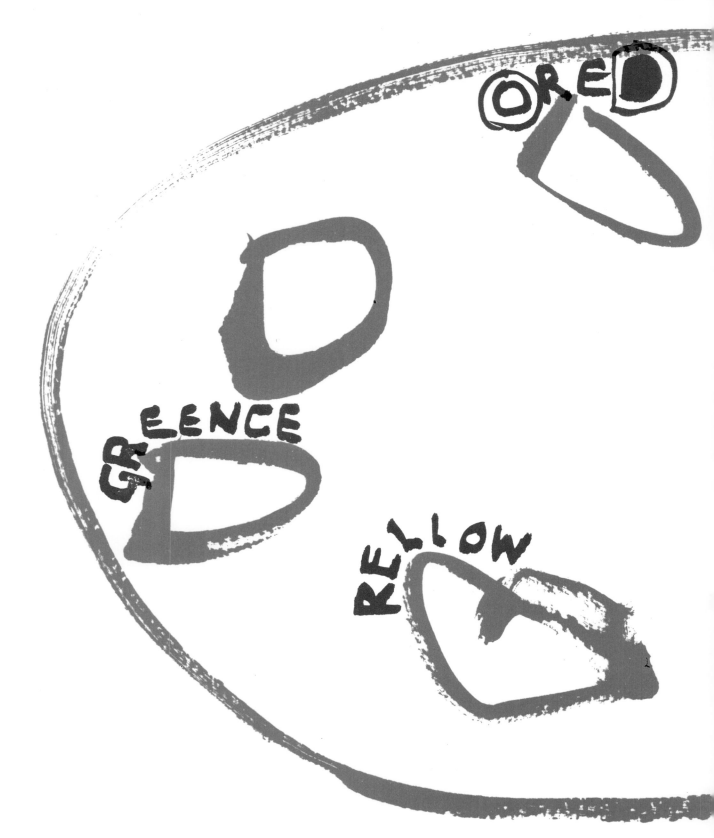

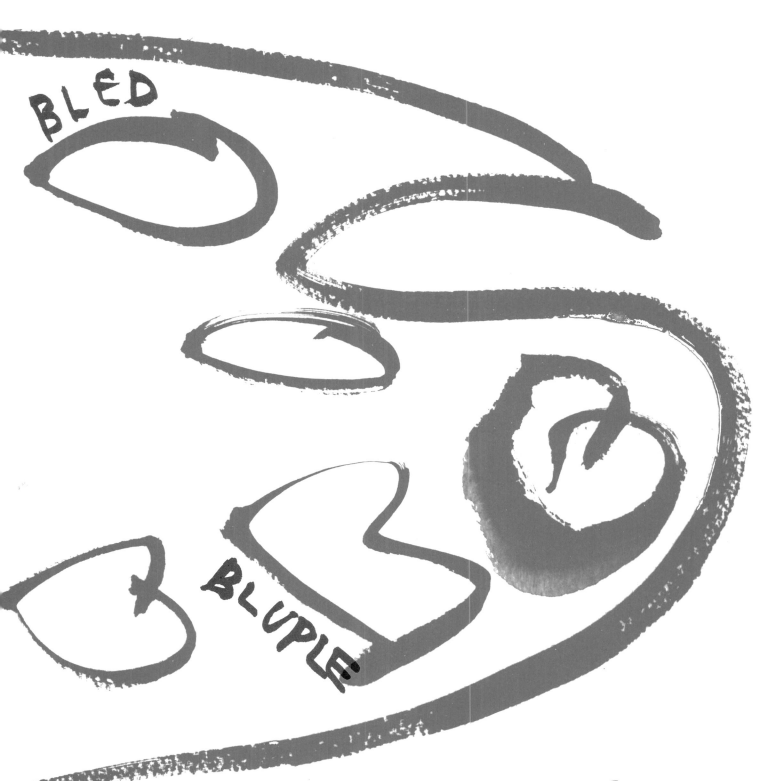

WORDS ARE
ART
WORDS ARE
POWERFUL

INVENT
NEW
WORDS

SPINGLE musple
Bilology STRAPNEY
GIPPY SEE TREE Pada
Ledap LAPLEAD
FETLA Neleza

What new words can you think of?

WHAT DO YOUR NEW WORDS MEAN? ARE THEY ADJECTIVES, NAMES, FEELINGS?

Paint their meanings here.

GIRAFFTOISE

MUSIC IS ART
FOR YOUR
EARS.

INVENT
THE LOOK OF
SOUNDS.

What would a dog's bark look like if you could see it?
What about a whisper or a laugh?

LET'S INVENT INSTRUMENTS

DRUMPET

CAN YOU PAINT HOW YOUR YOUR FAVOURITE SONG SOUNDS?

I LIKE THE SOUND OF THAT!

CAN YOU PAINT HOW YOUR VOICE SOUNDS?

CHAPTER 2.

PLAY IS POWERFUL

YOU CAN USE ART TO PLAY WITH COLOUR, SHAPE, WORDS AND ALMOST ANYTHING ELSE YOU CAN THINK OF.

ANYONE CAN PLAY WITH ART. ALL YOU NEED IS A SIMPLE WAY TO MAKE YOUR MARK, LIKE A PENCIL OR A PAINTBRUSH!

Try swishing, splatting, scribbling and scratching.

LET'S MAKE A LOOP DRAWING

Fill this page with lots and lots of looping lines.

THAT IS A LOOPY LOOP DRAWING

LET'S MAKE A DRAWING WITH YOUR EYES CLOSED

DRAW USING YOUR MIND'S EYE

I LIKE WHAT I SEE

LET'S TAKE A FOR A WALK

The artist Paul Klee said that drawing was like taking a line for a walk. How long can you keep your pencil on the page?

How many different
shapes and patterns
can your line make
on its walk?

LET'S TAKE A MARBLE FOR A ROLL

Try rolling a marble in paint
and then rolling it around on
the page. Or use a small ball,
if you don't have a marble.

You can try to make shapes and patterns, or just let the marble roll freely. You're making art either way!

THAT'S A GOOD ONE

LET'S TAKE A FINGER FOR A STROLL

Dip your finger in paint and walk it around these pages.
Where will it take you?

Try making your finger jump, slide and spin around!
What does that look like?

Draw two or more people having a conversation.
What are they saying? How are they feeling?

LET'S MAKE SOME WILD MARKS

WHAT CAN YOUR BRUSH DO?

DOTS · · ·
STRIPES
ZIGZAGS
SPLOTCHES . .

Try closing your eyes as you make your marks.
Surprise yourself with what you create!

PLAY WITH LETTERS

A B C D E F G H I J K L M N O P Q R S T U V W X Y Z

A font is a way of writing letters. Fonts are art. They make the same words look and feel different. See all the different ways these letters look?

Can you create your own font? Draw in the missing letters.
Then play around with colour, patterns and any other
effects you like to make the letters your own.

THAT IS A FANTASTIC FONT

ZAB

CDEFG

HIJKL

WRITE OUT
YOUR FINISHED
FONT HERE

WRITE YOUR NAME IN AS MANY DIFFERENT STYLES OR FONTS AS YOU CAN.

PRISHA

IGNACIO

CALEB

MUHAMMAD

EMILY

KRISHNA

MATEO

LIAM

SILAS

CARLOS

SOPHIA

JESSICA

MIA

FIERGAIL

ETTA

ABDULLAH

Fill this page with your name, as many times as you can fit in.

Try using different fonts to make your name look bouncy, angry, dreamy and powerful. Which of your fonts do you like best?

MAKE A PINK ON PINK PAINTING

You can paint and play with one colour to get to know it better.
Can you make it darker or paler?

What does the colour look like when you build it up in layers?
Or dribble, and splodge and write with it?

MIX IT UP

PLAY WITH COLOURS

Art lets you play with reality.
Try painting something in totally unreal colours.

NICE!

Maybe you could paint a blue banana? Or a pink and green cow?

IMAGINE THE WHOLE WORLD IN DIFFERENT COLOURS AND USE YOUR BRUSH OR PENCILS TO BRING IT TO LIIFE

Fill the world on these pages with all the 'wrong' colours. It's your art, and your world, so use whatever colours and patterns you like.

You can draw in extra details if you like
– and they can look however you want,
too. You're an artist – reality
can't tell you what to do!

HOW DO DIFFERENT COLOURS MAKE YOU FEEL?

BLUE

RED

PINK

Write or draw the first things that come into your head when you see these colours. It might be a feeling, memory, object or anything else.

Try painting or drawing other colours on these pages.
What do these colours make you think of?
Add words and drawings around them
to make more colour mind-maps.

YOU ARE SO COOL

HOW YOU DO FEEL RIGHT NOW?

Art can help us explore feelings and thoughts
that can be tricky to put into words.

What colour, or mix of colours,
best suits your mood right now?
Fill the space above with the colour of your mood.

Our moods change all the time. Try turning to another page
in this book and doing another activity, then come back to this page.
Fill the space below with the colour of your mood now.

Do your two works of mood art look different?
Try exploring your moods by keeping a wordless diary,
where you paint or draw how you feel each day.

PAINTINGS DON'T HAVE TO BE FLAT, OR REALISTIC, OR THE RIGHT WAY UP. ART GIVES YOU THE POWER TO MIX UP THE WORLD

WHY NOT BUILD UP YOUR PAINTINGS IN LAYERS LIKE A LETTUCE AND TOMATO SANDWICH?

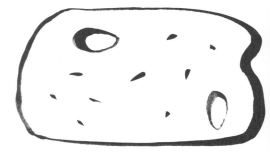

bread = paper

lettuce = paint

tomato = cut-up paper

This page is the first layer in your painting – the bread. Which layer do you want to add next? You can add as many layers as you like!

THAT LOOKS TASTY!

Turn this book upside down and start painting
what you can see out the window.

When you've finished, turn the book back the right way round.
You're seeing the world in a whole new way!

CAN YOU IMAGINE AN
UPSIDE DOWN WORLD?
YOU HAVE THE POWER TO
CREATE IT. NOW TURN YOUR
DRAWING THE OTHER WAY UP

Turn this book on its side and start painting the room you're in right now.

HOW ABOUT A
S-IDEWAYS

When you've finished, turn the book back round.
How does your sideways world make you feel?

WORLD?

DRAW YOURSELF FROM LOTS OF ANGLES AT ONCE LIKE PABLO PICASSO

Pablo Picasso was a Spanish modern artist.
He often painted faces as if you could see them from
above, below, straight-ahead and side all at once.

You can start by drawing your face as you see it in the mirror.
Then imagine seeing yourself from above, below and side-on.
Draw those versions of your face on top of what you've already drawn!

PABLO WOULD BE PROUD

VISIT THE SHAPE INVENTION CENTER

INVENT A WILD NEW SHAPE

How many sides does your shape have?
Does it have straight lines, or curves or both?

GIVE IT A NAME

· · · · · · · · · · · · · · · · ·

HOW MANY SQUARES CAN YOU FIT IN THERE?

Fill these squares with smaller squares.
Follow the example or do it your own way.

LET'S DRAW A CRYSTAL

NOW CARRY ON

Grow your crystal by adding triangles that touch on at least one side. Can you make it fill the whole page?

HOW MANY CIRCLES CAN YOU FIT IN ?

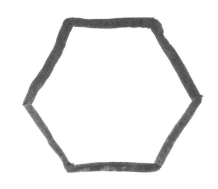

HOW MANY
HEXAGONS
CAN YOU
FIT IN ?

IN THE SHAPE ENCLOSURE

Draw shapes in the wild. Are they hunting alone or running in packs?
Or maybe they're flying?

You can add a few words to describe what the shapes are all doing.

NOW FILL YOUR BOWL WITH PASTA SHAPES

squiggle

square

Draw a big, tasty pile of squiggles, squares, triangles and tubes in your giant bowl.

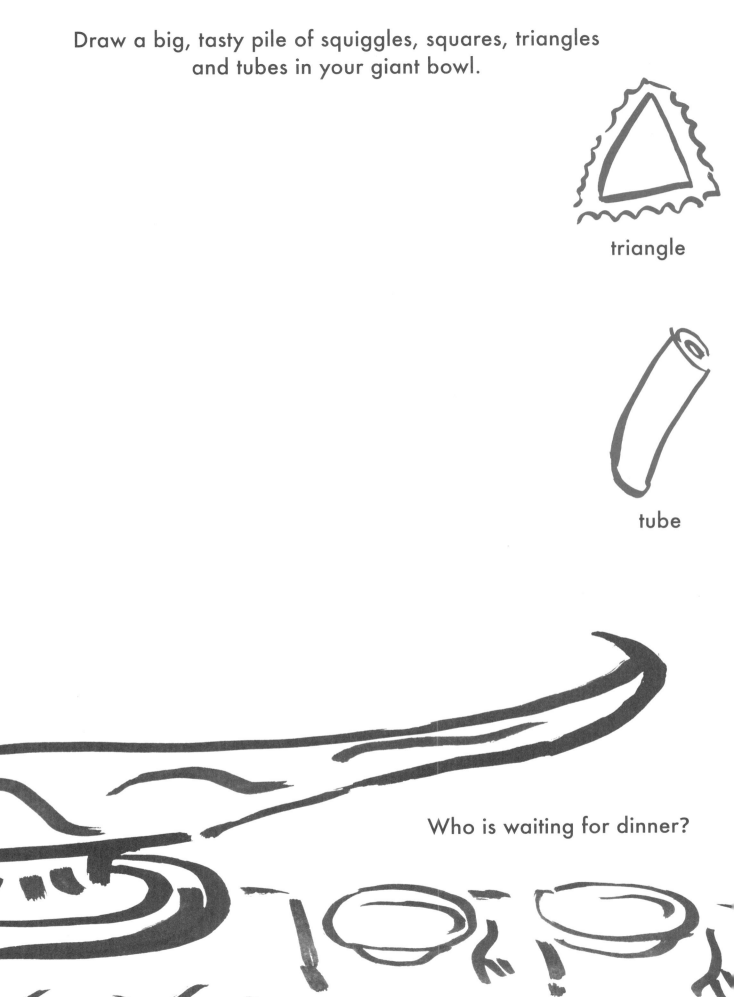

triangle

tube

Who is waiting for dinner?

LET'S TESSELATE

WHEN SHAPES TESSELATE
IT MEANS THEY FIT
TOGETHER JUST RIGHT

Create a tesselating pattern and draw faces on the shapes to bring it to life!

You can start with simple shapes, like triangles and squares.
Then make up some shapes of your own.
Remember, circles don't tesselate!

CREATE A PATTERN AND BRING IT TO LIFE.

▶ FILL THIS SPACE WITH ALL THE SHAPES YOU CAN THINK OF. . . .

Can you create patterns from your shapes?

How about drawing some shapes within shapes?
Like a triangle inside a circle, or a star inside a square?

I LIKE HOW YOU ARE THROWING THOSE SHAPES

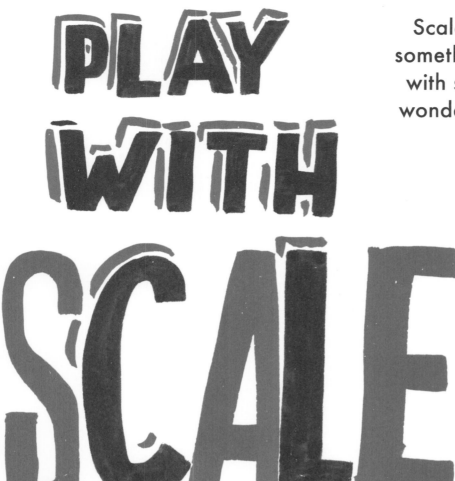

PLAY WITH SCALE

Scale means how big or small something is. In art, you can play with scale to make strange and wonderful versions of our world.

Draw yourself here, reacting to this strangely huge thing.

Here, draw something huge that is usually tiny.
It could be a beetle, a kitten or anything else you like.

WHAT ABOUT MAKING SOMETHING VERY SOMETHING VERY HUGE, VERY VERY SMALL?

Art gives you the power to shrink down huge things to fit in the palm of your hand. What would you like to hold and look at up close?

Draw around your hand. Then draw something inside it that is usually massive. A blue whale, a skyscraper or a rocket?
Make it as detailed as you can.

ART DOESN'T HAVE TO BE PERFECT OR SERIOUS OR TAKE A LONG TIME. LET'S MAKE FUN, FAST ART

Set a timer for 10 seconds and draw your face. Ready... go!

Put another 10 seconds on the clock and draw your favourite food.
Don't think, just draw!

This time, don't try to draw anything in particuar. Put 10 seconds on the clock, then just let your hand make whatever shapes it wants. Set it free!

SO FAST!

ART CAN ALSO BE -S·L·O·W-

Try to use all sorts of different lines to join the dots. Could you make them spiky, curved, dotted or loopy? Or maybe they could be made of lots of tiny triangles or squares?

How many different colours can you use?
Try colouring in all the shapes, one by one.

Relax and see where your mind takes you.

BREAK ALL THE RULES.

Great artists love breaking the rules and seeing what happens.

Instead of painting with your hands, like most artists do,
why not use your feet? Or your elbows? Or your knees?

YOUR TURN NOW

ART GIVES YOU THE POWER TO MAKE UP YOUR OWN RULES

Look out the window at the world outside. Then write four rules for how things will be different to 'the real world' in your drawing.

1.
2.
3.
4.

In your art, anything is possible. Cats can be as big as trees, everyone's hair can be blue, you can climb to the Moon on a spiral staircase, and the rain can be made of marshmallows.

Fill this page with a drawing that breaks the 'real world's' rules and uses your four new arty rules instead.

CHAPTER 3.
PEOPLE ARE POWERFUL

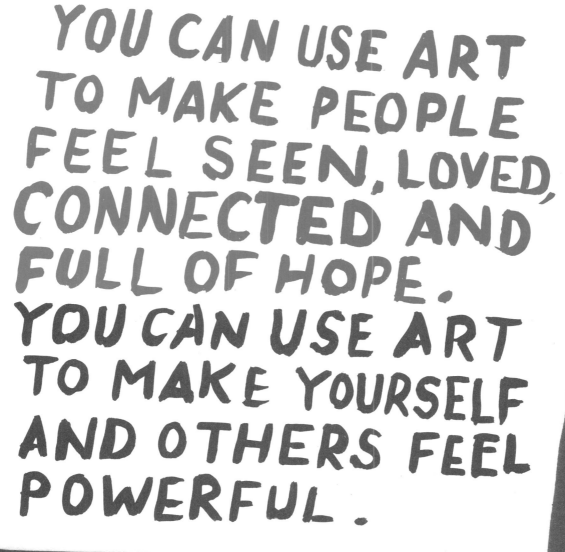

YOU CAN USE ART TO MAKE PEOPLE FEEL SEEN, LOVED, CONNECTED AND FULL OF HOPE. YOU CAN USE ART TO MAKE YOURSELF AND OTHERS FEEL POWERFUL.

ART IS YOUR HUMAN RIGHT

YOU HAVE THE RIGHT TO MAKE AND ENJOY ART!

DRAW YOURSELF MAKING ART

You could draw yourself painting a huge mural
on a wall, making a sculpture out of rubbish
or doing anything else you feel like!

NOW DRAW YOURSELF IN HERE

YOU!

Try closing your eyes and picturing your face. Are you smiling? Laughing? Looking serious? You could draw that – or how you feel right now.

ART CAN TELL PEOPLE ABOUT YOU

Use colours, lines and shapes to show how
dancing or singing or doing anything else makes you FEEL!
How you feel tells people a lot about you, too.

HOW DO YOU... WALK?

PARTY? DANCE? SING?

If you're not sure how you do these things,
or how you feel doing them, get up and give them a try!

HOW DO YOU... DRESS? TALK? EAT? LIVE?

Try starting to paint without thinking too much about what you're doing. Let your brain surprise you!

What are your favourite clothes? Things to eat?
People, or animals to talk to? Fun moments in your day?

I LIKE YOUR STYLE

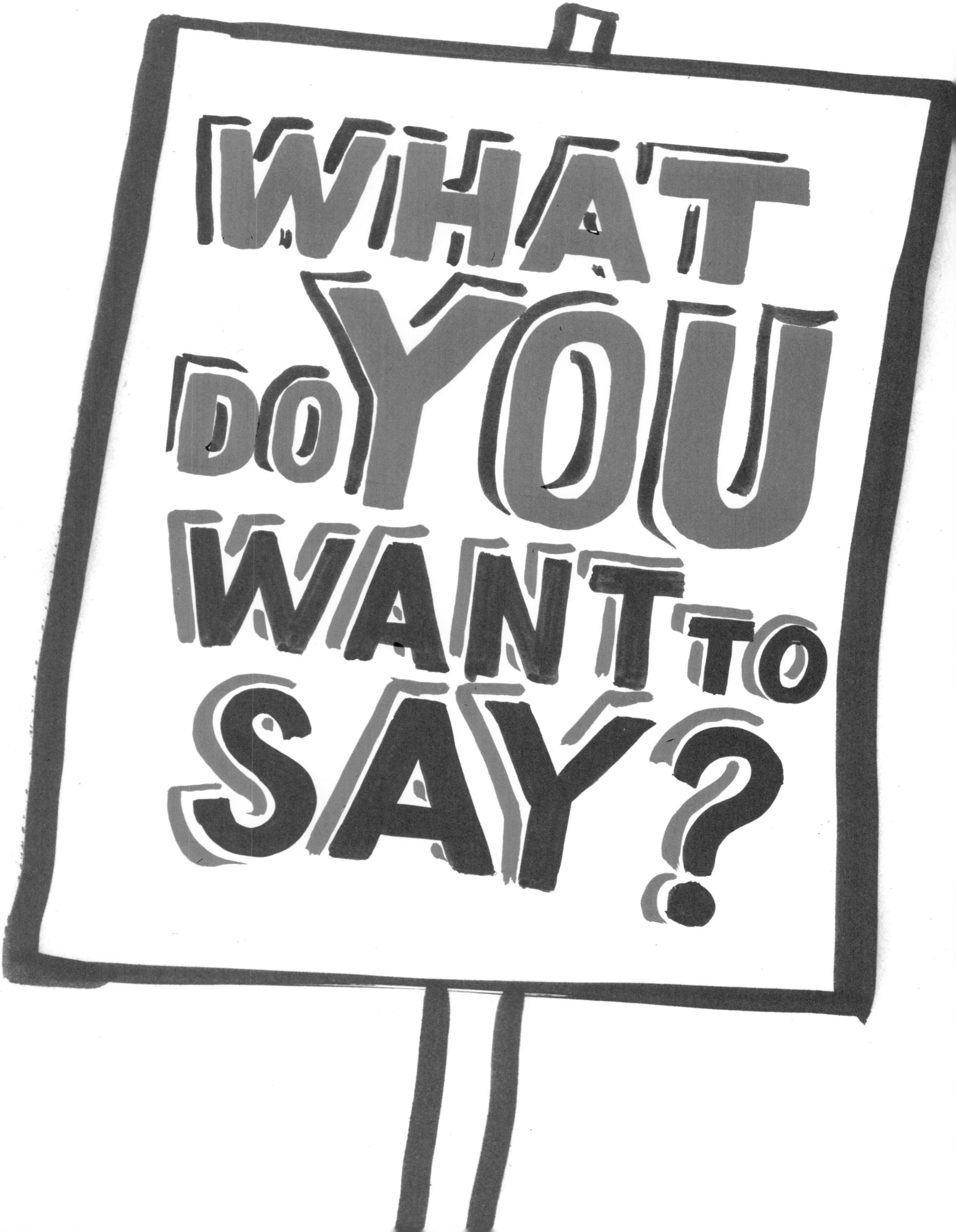
WHAT DO YOU WANT TO SAY?

Write or draw what you most want to tell the world.

YOU TELL THEM!

ART
HELPS
YOU
GROW

What do you want to draw growing here? It doesn't have to be a plant!

WHAT'S IN THAT PLANT POT?

ART FEEDS YOUR DREAMS

Pile that plate high with your drawing! Do you want to fill
it with food, or something else?

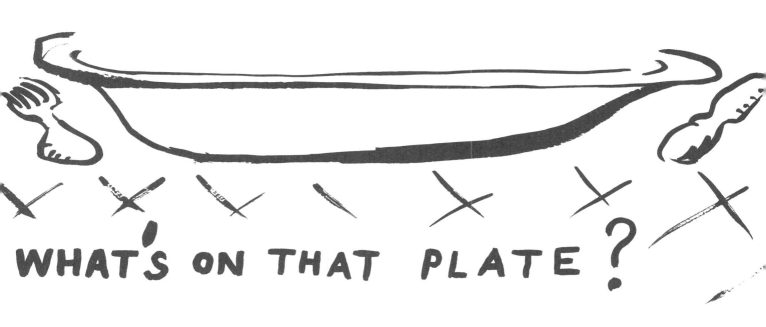

WHAT'S ON THAT PLATE?

ART TELLS STORIES

Use your pencil or paintbrush to tell the story of how you learned to make art. What memories do you have? Who helped you learn?

What stories do you want to tell other people
through your art? Draw or paint some of them here.

IMAGINE A

What would a better world look like to you? Draw it here.

BETTER WORLD

Art gives people the power to see a better world.
How could you help make the world you've drawn a reality?

CREATE A PIECE OF ART THAT MAKES YOU FEEL CONFIDENT AND POWERFUL

What are some words or pictures that encourage and inspire you?
How can you use them here?

Fill this space with your powerful art!
Use your favourite colours, patterns and shapes.

What are your favourite things about the people you love?
See if you can show them in your art.

Who are the people you love? Draw or paint them here.

HOW MUCH LOVE CAN YOU PUT IN A PAINTING ?

Fill all the hearts with colour and pattern. Will you decorate them all the same way, or make each one look completely different?

Don't forget about the space between the hearts.
Do you want to fill it with more hearts?
Or maybe something else that makes you think of love?

MAKE A PAINTING AS A PRESENT FOR SOMEONE YOU LOVE

What will your painting show? It could be you and the person you're giving the painting to. Or maybe it could include some of their favourite things?

Don't forget the frame! You could make your gift even more special by decorating it with colours and patterns.

THESE TWO PAINTINGS LOVE EACH OTHER

BUT WHO OR WHAT IS IN THEM?

Do you want your paintings to talk to each other? You could paint words – or is there another way they could talk?

How will someone be able to tell that these paintings love each other? Try making it as obvious as you can!

THERE is STILL ART, THERE IS STILL HOPE

WHAT DO YOU THINK IS HOPEFUL?

You could paint one big thing that gives you hope, or lots of different things. If you'd prefer to write your answer, try painting the words.

HOPE MAKES PEOPLE POWERFUL. CREATE A PAINTING OF HOPE FOR SOMEONE WHO NEEDS CHEERING UP

What colours and shapes feel hopeful to you?

THAT IS A HOPEFUL IMAGE!

HOW DOES ART MAKE YOU POWERFUL? ARTISTS ANNI AND JOSEPH ALBERS THOUGHT ART ASKED YOU TO LOOK AT the WORLD, THINK, AND THEN TAKE ACTION.

Spend a few minute looking out of the window. What did you notice? Create a piece of art to share what you saw with others.

It can be really powerful to show how they felt to you, or to add in other things that they remind you of. For instance, a plastic bag blowing in the wind might make you think of a sailboat or a hot-air balloon!

WHAT CAN YOU SEE IN THIS SCRIBBLE? HOW DOES IT MAKE YOU FEEL?

People all experience the world in different ways.
Art is powerful because it helps to show us that.

Ask someone else to look at the scribble and blot on these pages
and tell you what they see and feel. It might surprise you!

WHAT DO YOU SEE AND FEEL WHEN YOU LOOK AT THESE INK BLOTS?

Scribble, drip and smudge paint onto the page, without trying to make it look like anything in particular.

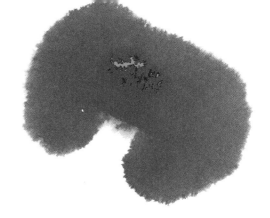

Can you see an object or a face or anything else in it?
Ask other people what they see and feel when they look at it.

EVERYONE HAS CULTURE

Our culture is the way we share our life and our stories.
Food, festivals, clothes and art are all part of our culture.
Draw something from your culture that you love.

Culture is powerful because it brings us together. Show this drawing to someone you love. See what feelings and memories it inspires in them.

ART HAS THE POWER TO

All of our faces are unique. Eyes, ears, noses and mouths can look all sorts of ways. Try to fill this space with as many different ones as you can – including your own!

MAKE PEOPLE FEEL SEEN

Don't forget to include things like bumps, scars, moles, piercings and hairs.
There are all sorts of ways that we can look different from each other.

THESE HEADS NEED FACES

CAN YOU HELP?

Use a wide range of different features for your faces. You can turn back to the previous page and look at all the fantastic features you drew there.

Try creating faces that show different emotions.
Happy, sad, angry, shocked – anything you like!

Look at all these faces!
Fill in the spaces with your own painted faces.

Can you think up names and characters for the faces you've drawn here? Give each person a special power!

ART HAS THE POWER TO

CAN YOU HELP?

Who is this person? Paint them here and show them who they are.

ANSWER BIG QUESTIONS

And who is this?
Finish the painting
and show them
the powerful things
they can do!

WE ARE POWERFUL WHEN WE ARE CONNECTED

THIS IS A MAP OF MY CONNECTIONS

HOW ARE YOU CONNECTED TO OTHER PEOPLE?

What connects you to these people? Maybe on a basic level they are 'friend' or 'aunt'. But what else? Maybe you both like art, or football or you have the same favourite animal. Write this on your map.

DRAW YOUR OWN CONNECTION MAP

Which towns or cities and countries do your friends and family live in? You can write in where in the world they are.

WHAT CAN YOU DO WITH OTHERS?

MAKE A PAINTING TOGETHER!

FORM A DANCE TROUPE?

WRITE A SONG!

DRESS UP

Making art with other people is powerful. Draw some ideas here for what you could do together. Then you can choose the one that looks the most fun, and ask someone to do it with you.

PEOPLE POWER!

Paint a crowd of powerful people using art to change the world.
What are they saying?

Write and draw
powerful messages
onto the placards
these protesters
are holding.

DRAW THE WHOLE WORLD IN YOUR HAND

How does it feel to see the Earth in your hand?
How will you use your power to enjoy and protect our planet?

THAT IS A BEAUTIFUL WORLD FOR YOU TO EXPLORE

Art has the power to remind people that we are all connected to Earth, as well as to each other.

People are powerful enough to save our world. Art helps people step into their power, find their voice, and inspire others to do the same.

Fill this half of the page with words and pictures that inspire you.

Now in this half of the page, squeeze all that inspiration into your own piece of art. You could use words or pictures, or both. What do you want to say? Inspire others with your voice!

Life force fills us with energy, excitement and imagination.
Paint how it feels when you're charged up with life force.

What makes you feel charged up with life force? Maybe it's nature, or playing or music? Whatever it is for you, draw or paint it here.

Try your hardest to show how excited and energised it makes you feel, so people looking at your art can feel that too!

USE ART TO SPREAD YOUR LIFEFORCE ACROSS THE UNIVERSE

Draw yourself here. See those waves?
That is your life force! Continue drawing waves
spreading out across these pages.

LOOKING GOOD

You can fill your waves of life force with all sorts of colours and patterns.
Try to make the waves look really exciting and full of creative energy.

YOU HAVE JOINED A GROUP OF AMAZING PEOPLE ABLE TO LOOK AND LISTEN TO THE UNIVERSE AND MAKE THINGS HAPPEN!

THIS BOOK IS DEDICATED TO ETTA FERGAL JESSICA

BOB AND ROBERTA SMITH

First Published in 2023 by Wide Eyed Editions,
an imprint of The Quarto Group, 1 Triptych Place, London, SE1 9SH.
T (0)20 7700 6700 F (0)20 7700 8066 **www.Quarto.com**
WTS TAX d.o.o., Žanova ulica 3, 4000 Kranj, Slovenija. www.wts-tax.si

A catalogue record for this book is available from the British Library.

ISBN 978-0-7112-6539-4

The artwork in this book was hand painted
Set in Futura

Published by Debbie Foy
Commissioned by Lucy Brownridge
Edited by Alice Harman
Designed by Belinda Webster and Kate Haynes
Production by Elizabeth Reardon

Manufactured in Guangdong, China TT082023

9 8 7 6 5 4 3 2

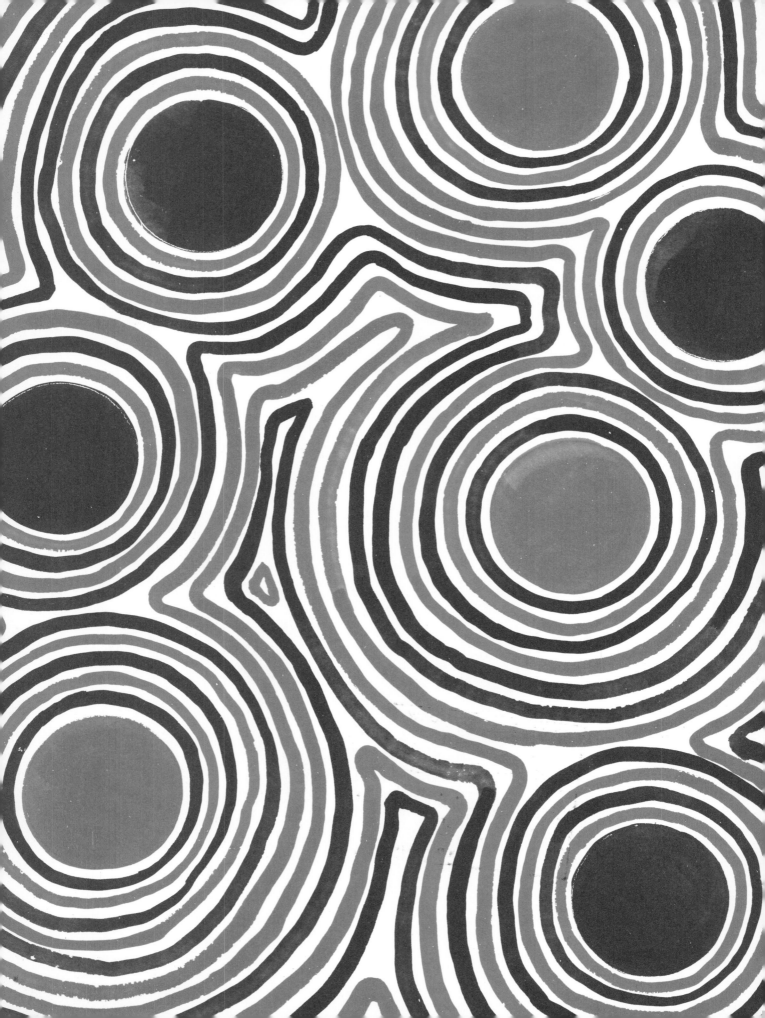